WHY DO FROGS HAVE TEETH?

AND OTHER CURIOUS AMPHIBIAN ADAPTATIONS

BY PATRICIA FLETCHER

Gareth Stevens
PUBLISHING

Please visit our website, www.garethstevens.com. For a free color catalog of all our high-quality books, call toll free 1-800-542-2595 or fax 1-877-542-2596.

Cataloging-in-Publication Data

Names: Fletcher, Patricia.
Title: Why do frogs have teeth? And other curious amphibian adaptations / Patricia Fletcher.
Description: New York : Gareth Stevens Publishing, 2018. | Series: Odd adaptations | Includes index.
Identifiers: ISBN 9781538203897 (pbk.) | ISBN 9781538203910 (library bound) | ISBN 9781538203903 (6 pack)
Subjects: LCSH: Frogs–Juvenile literature. | Adaptation (Biology)–Juvenile literature.
Classification: LCC QL668.E2 F54 2018 | DDC 597.8'9–dc23

First Edition

Published in 2018 by
Gareth Stevens Publishing
111 East 14th Street, Suite 349
New York, NY 10003

Copyright © 2018 Gareth Stevens Publishing

Designer: Sarah Liddell
Editor: Kristen Nelson

Photo credits: Cover, p. 1 Education Images/Contributor/Universal Images Group/Getty Images; background used throughout Captblack76/Shutterstock.com; p. 4 sergey0506/Shutterstock.com; p. 5 (main) Greg Nesbit Photography/Shutterstock.com; p. 5 (caecilian) kamnuan/Shutterstock.com; p. 6 Nicholas Toh/Shutterstock.com; p. 7 Kazakova Maryia/Shutterstock.com; p. 8 Dein Freund der Baum/Wikimedia Commons; pp. 9, 27 Daniel Mietchen/Wikimedia Commons; p. 10 Steve Byland/Shutterstock.com; p. 11 Jay Ondreicka/Shutterstock.com; p. 12 Gerald A. DeBoer/Shutterstock.com; p. 13 Joe Farah/Shutterstock.com; p. 14 Kuttelvaserova Stuchelova/Shutterstock.com; p. 15 lumen-digital/Shutterstock.com; p. 16 reptiles4all/Shutterstock.com; p. 17 (top) Michael McCoy/Getty Images; p. 17 (bottom) Martin Harvey/Getty Images; p. 18 Aleksey Stemmer/Shutterstock.com; p. 19 davemhuntphotography/Shutterstock.com; p. 20 WathanyuSowong/Shutterstock.com; p. 21 Howcheng/Wikimedia Commons; p. 22 LifetimeStock/Shutterstock.com; p. 23 Lubomir Dajc/Shutterstock.com; p. 24 xpixel/Shutterstock.com; p. 25 Freebilly/Shutterstock.com; p. 26 Josve05a/Wikimedia Commons; p. 29 Juliann/Shutterstock.com.

Printed in China

CPSIA compliance information: Batch #CS17GS: For further information contact Gareth Stevens, New York, New York at 1-800-542-2595.

CONTENTS

Words in the glossary appear in **bold** type the first time they are used in the text.

ADAPTABLE AMPHIBIANS

Amphibians are some of the coolest—and weirdest—animals on Earth! They include any animal with a backbone that spends time living both in water and on land during their life. There are about 7,500 species, or kinds, of amphibians alive today.

AMPHIBIANS FALL INTO THREE MAIN GROUPS:
- FROGS AND TOADS: NO TAIL, WIDE BODY, LONG BACK LEGS
- NEWTS AND SALAMANDERS: TAIL, SLENDER BODY, TWO PAIRS OF LEGS
- CAECILIANS (SIH-*SIHL*-YUHNZ): NO LEGS, WORMLIKE

Amphibians have some really strange adaptations that have allowed them to survive for millions of years. Some of these adaptations are present in most amphibians. Other behaviors and body adaptations have been **developed** only by certain species.

FROG

"AMPHIBIAN" COMES FROM A GREEK WORD MEANING "LIVING A DOUBLE LIFE." HOWEVER, SOME ADULT AMPHIBIANS LIVE ONLY IN THE WATER AND OTHERS ONLY ON LAND.

NEWT

ADAPT TO LIVE

An adaptation is a change in an animal's body or behavior that makes it better suited to its surroundings. An adaptation might make it a better hunter or able to hide from predators more easily. The ability to adapt can mean the difference between an animal surviving or dying out altogether!

CAECILIAN

5

INSIDE THE CYCLE

One of the oddest adaptations of amphibians is their life cycle! Most amphibians lay eggs that hatch into larvae that live in water. The larvae grow lungs and often legs to live on land. After a time, they become adults and start the cycle over again!

Many adaptations exist within this life cycle. For example, some amphibian eggs hatch in days, while others hatch in weeks! **SOME AMPHIBIANS LAY EGGS COVERED IN A STICKY COATING.** This protects the eggs and lets them stick to plants and not be carried away by the water. Other amphibian females carry their eggs on their back!

FROG EGGS

6

GOOD PARENTING

Most amphibian parents do something to keep their eggs safe. Some work extra hard! Male and female spiny salamanders take turns curling around their eggs and turning them over. Some kinds of newts wrap their eggs in leaves—and they may lay up to 450 eggs at a time!

THIS ILLUSTRATION SHOWS THE LIFE CYCLE OF A FROG, WHICH IS SIMILAR TO MANY OTHER AMPHIBIANS' LIFE CYCLE.

ADULT FROGS BREATHE AIR, HAVE FOUR LEGS, AND NO TAIL.

EGGS ARE LAID BY A FEMALE FROG.

FROGLETS HAVE ALL FOUR LEGS. THEIR TAIL STARTS TO GET SHORTER.

FROGS START TO GROW A TAIL WHILE THEY'RE STILL INSIDE THE EGG.

TADPOLES START TO GROW LEGS.

THE EGGS HATCH AS TADPOLES THAT BREATHE THROUGH GILLS AND HAVE A TAIL.

7

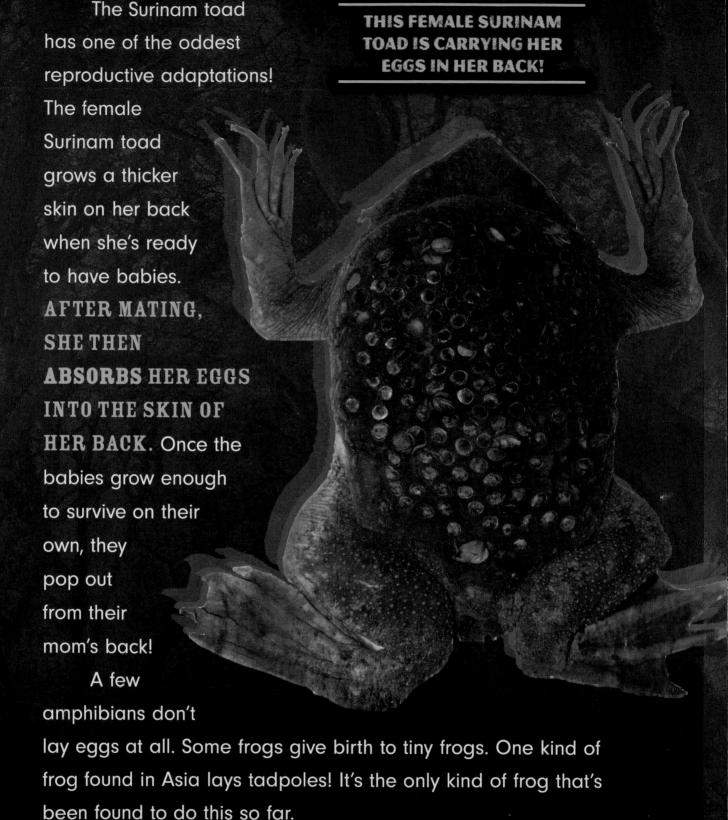

The Surinam toad has one of the oddest reproductive adaptations! The female Surinam toad grows a thicker skin on her back when she's ready to have babies. **AFTER MATING, SHE THEN ABSORBS HER EGGS INTO THE SKIN OF HER BACK.** Once the babies grow enough to survive on their own, they pop out from their mom's back!

A few amphibians don't lay eggs at all. Some frogs give birth to tiny frogs. One kind of frog found in Asia lays tadpoles! It's the only kind of frog that's been found to do this so far.

THIS FEMALE SURINAM TOAD IS CARRYING HER EGGS IN HER BACK!

WEIRD "WORM" BABIES

Depending on the species, caecilians may lay eggs or give birth to live young. When caecilian larvae do hatch from eggs, they live in water and even have a tail with fins to help them swim! Once they grow into adults, they leave the water and live underground.

CAECILIAN EGGS

All amphibians are cold-blooded. That means their body temperature depends on their **environment**. Because of this, some amphibians have had to adapt to **extreme** heat or cold where they live.

THE SPRING PEEPER FROG, WOOD FROG, AND SOME OTHER FROGS USE AN "ANTIFREEZE" IN THEIR BODY TO KEEP FROM FREEZING TO DEATH DURING WINTER!

These frogs may shelter under leaf litter or squeeze themselves into cracks in wood and rocks to wait out the cold. They don't move. Their heart stops beating, and they even stop breathing! They start moving again when it warms up.

WOOD FROG

Amphibians live all over the world in different environments they've adapted to. They live in trees, near lakes, on forest floors, and more. However, they don't live in Earth's icy polar regions. These are too cold for too much of the year for amphibians!

AMPHIBIANS LIVE IN ALL SORTS OF ENVIRONMENTS. SPRING PEEPER FROGS LIKE THIS ONE ARE FOUND IN EASTERN NORTH AMERICA.

Amphibians have adapted to very hot, dry weather, too! Some desert amphibians have sped up their life cycle so they can take advantage of the short-lived pools of water made by summer storms. Couch's spadefoot toads go to these pools, mate, and eat all in one night. Then, their eggs hatch in just 2 weeks!

COAT OF SKIN?

The African bullfrog also estivates during dry times of the year. It **sheds** some of its skin, but keeps it on to make a "raincoat." **INSTEAD OF KEEPING RAIN OUT, THE BULLFROG'S HOMEMADE RAINCOAT KEEPS THE WATER IN THEIR BODY IN!** The dry season can last months. The bullfrogs lose their extra skin when the rain starts again.

LIKE MANY DESERT AMPHIBIANS, THE CALIFORNIA TIGER SALAMANDER STAYS IN A BURROW DURING THE DRIEST TIME OF YEAR. It becomes inactive, much like the freezing frogs! This period of inactivity is called estivation. Once it rains, the salamander wakes up and carries on eating and living as usual.

CALIFORNIA TIGER SALAMANDER

12

SPADEFOOT TOADS LIKE THIS ONE ALSO HAVE A SPECIAL BODY PART ON THEIR BACK FEET THAT HELPS THEM DIG THE HOLES THEY USE TO KEEP COOL.

13

DON'T HOLD YOUR BREATH!

Many amphibians have a thin skin that's moist, or feels wet. **BUT IT'S MORE THAN JUST A BODY COVERING. AMPHIBIANS CAN BREATHE THROUGH THEIR SKIN!** In order to absorb oxygen into their skin, the skin must stay moist. That's why many amphibians make a slimy matter called mucus, which they **release** and let cover their skin. The oxygen goes right into **blood vessels** to move around the body!

Amphibian larvae take in oxygen through gills when they're growing in the water. Most then develop lungs to breathe with as they become adults and use those as well as their skin to breathe.

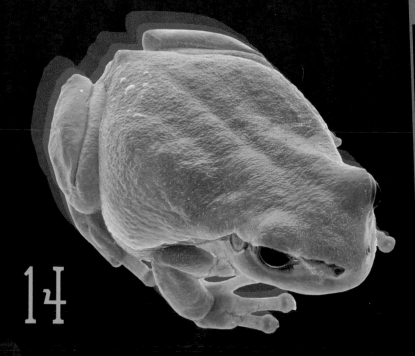

ONE FOR ONE

When amphibians breathe through their skin, it's called cutaneous gas exchange. "Cutaneous" means "of the skin." As they take in oxygen, they're giving off carbon dioxide—or "exchanging" one gas for the other. The blood vessels they use for this are found very close to the surface of their skin to make the exchange work.

FROGS USE THEIR LUNGS FOR ANOTHER PURPOSE, TOO. THEY FILL THEIR LUNGS TO HELP THEM FLOAT A BIT AS THEY SWIM!

HIDDEN IN PLAIN SIGHT

Have you ever tried to spot a toad by the edge of a pond? It can be hard—until it jumps in the water! **TOADS ARE A BROWNISH-GREEN COLOR, JUST LIKE THE MUDDY PLACES THEY LIKE TO LIVE.** Using color and **texture** to blend in with surroundings is called camouflage. It's an adaptation that allows many amphibians to hide from predators and surprise prey.

The Mindanao horned frog takes camouflage one step further. It's not just the same color of the leaves it lives on. Its body has leaf-like shapes on it that make it even harder to see! It may even sit still as a leaf so it stays hidden.

SALAMANDER

SNEAKY SALAMANDERS

Salamanders are nocturnal, or mostly active at night. To better hide from predators, salamanders are darker colors. What's more, if a predator does catch them, some kinds of salamanders can lose their tail. The tail keeps moving to confuse the predator while the salamander escapes! Afterward, the salamander regrows its tail.

CAN YOU SPOT ALL THE CAMOUFLAGED FROGS IN THESE PICTURES?

PRETTY—BUT POISONOUS!

While some amphibians use their skin to hide, others use their skin to stand out! They're brightly colored to let predators know they're poisonous.

If you're ever traveling in the rainforest on the coast of Colombia, stay away from a bright yellow frog. **THE GOLDEN POISON DART FROG IS TINY, BUT IT'S ONE OF THE MOST POISONOUS ANIMALS ON EARTH!** While one of these 1-inch (2.5 cm) frogs has enough poison in it to kill 10 people, it only gives off this special toxin when it's scared. Its coloring, which can range from bright yellow to green and orange, is a sure warning to predators.

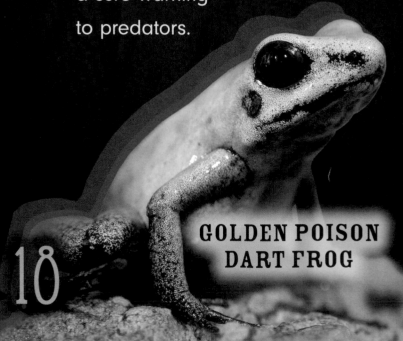

GOLDEN POISON DART FROG

POISON FROM PREY?

Scientists think poison dart frogs, including the golden poison dart frog, might get their poison from their prey that eat certain plants. When they're raised outside of their rainforest home, golden poison dart frogs aren't poisonous at all! In the wild, poison dart frogs have one predator that isn't affected by their poison, a South American snake.

TREE FROGS ARE KNOWN
FOR BEING QUITE COLORFUL
TO REMIND PREDATORS THEY
AREN'T GOOD TO EAT!

19

THE ROUGH-SKINNED NEWT MAKES SO MUCH POISON, IT COULD KILL A ROOM FULL OF PEOPLE!

While all newts make some kind of poison to keep safe, the rough-skinned newt has had to adapt to make more than most other newts. Why? Garter snakes, the rough-skinned newt's main predator, have **evolved** to be able to survive the kind of poison the newt makes.

Over time, the newts that have made the most poison have survived garter snakes. But this allows only the garter snakes most resistant to the poison to survive to pass on their genes, forcing the most poisonous newts to keep up!

WHICH IS A NEWT?

All newts are salamanders, but not all salamanders are newts. They're all part of the animal group Caudata. Within Caudata, newts are part of the animal family Salamandridae. However, salamanders and newts share many features and adaptations. It's hard to tell them apart without a little **research**!

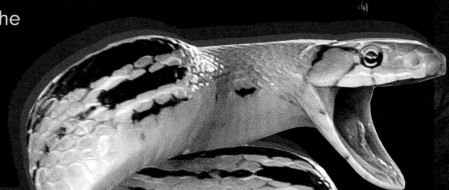

ROUGH-SKINNED NEWTS GIVE OFF THE SAME KIND OF POISON BLOWFISH DO!

21

THAT'S THE TOOTH!

Adult amphibians are carnivores, which means they eat meat. Some feast on bugs and worms, and those living in water may even eat small fish. Surely you've seen a picture of a frog shooting a sticky tongue out to catch its prey! **BUT DID YOU KNOW THAT A FROG USES TEETH TO KEEP THE PREY IT CATCHES? IN FACT, ALMOST ALL FROGS HAVE TEETH!**

A frog's teeth are tough to see unless you get close. They're found on the upper jaw and roof of a frog's mouth. These work with their tongue to keep a good hold on food frogs catch.

PIXIE FROG

FROGS LOSE THEIR TEETH THROUGHOUT THEIR LIFE. AS THEY LOSE ONE, A NEW ONE GROWS IN ITS PLACE!

A TOOTHY TREE FROG

Only one kind of frog has been found to have teeth on its upper and lower jaw: the South American marsupial tree frog. Other frogs have bigger teeth on their upper jaw and tooth-like spikes on their lower jaw, but those aren't real teeth.

23

GETTING JUMPY

Do you move differently when walking the halls of school than when running on the soccer field? That's a bit like adapting to your environment! Amphibian movement has developed to match where amphibians live, too.

With their long back legs, frog bodies seem made to jump. **NOT ALL FROGS JUMP THE SAME WAY!** Frogs that live in trees can jump high, but they don't go very far with each jump. Frogs that live in water can jump far, but much lower to the ground. Frogs that burrow can't jump very high or very far. Still, some frogs don't jump much! They walk or hop to get around.

TREE FROG

THAT'LL STICK!

Some frogs can do more than jump—they can stick! The pads on tree frogs' toes give off a matter that allows frogs to stick to many surfaces. They also have tiny parts on the toe pads called nanopillars that are specially shaped to keep them from falling.

FROGS' BODIES HAVE ADAPTED OVER TIME IN SOME ODD AND AMAZING WAYS!

THE MYSTERY AMPHIBIAN

Scientists haven't been studying caecilians as much or as long as other amphibians because, for a time, they were simply hard to find! These amphibians burrow underground, an adaptation they likely developed to hide from predators. ONE THING SCIENTISTS DO KNOW: IN ORDER TO BURROW AS WELL AS CAECILIANS DO, THEY NEED TO BE REALLY STRONG!

Caecilians have **ancestors** in common with other amphibians, but over millions of years, they lost their legs and tail, and their skull got stronger and thicker. They use their skull to push through the soil and move underground. CAECILIANS CAN PUSH THROUGH SOIL ABOUT TWO TIMES HARDER THAN SOME SNAKES!

CAECILIANS HAVE TWO IMPORTANT **TENDONS** THAT WORK WITH THEIR MUSCLES TO PUSH THROUGH SOIL WHILE BURROWING.

STRANGE DINNERS

Adult caecilians like to eat earthworms and crickets—but caecilian babies eat pieces of their mom! The mother caecilian's topmost layer of skin has extra fat in it. The layer is already dead, so when the babies climb on her and snack on it, it doesn't harm her. No other animals feed their young this way!

KEEP CHANGING

Amphibians have been surviving on Earth for millions of years. They've been able to adapt as the environments on our planet changed. Though the dinosaurs didn't survive, amphibians did!

However, today many amphibians are endangered, or in danger of dying out. Climate change is slowly altering Earth's weather patterns and changing where amphibians live in ways that harm them. They're losing their homes to people constructing roads and buildings. Pollution, too, greatly harms amphibians of all kinds.

Scientists think that Earth may be changing too fast now for amphibians to adapt. Then again, they've been developing odd adaptations for millions of years—maybe amphibians will find a way to adapt again!

GLOBAL SICKNESS

Amphibians all over the world are dying from an illness called chytridiomycosis (ky-trih-dee-oh-my-KOH-suhs). It stops amphibians from being able to properly take in oxygen and water through their skin. The sickness wasn't discovered until the 1990s and continues to spread quickly through amphibians. Scientists are hard at work to try to fight the illness.

AMPHIBIANS IN DANGER!

BARACOA
DWARF FROG
(CUBA)

BLUNT-HEADED
SALAMANDER
(MEXICO)

PUERTO RICAN
CRESTED TOAD
(PUERTO RICO)

CHINESE GIANT
SALAMANDER
(CHINA)

SAGALLA
CAECILIAN
(KENYA)

PANAMANIAN
GOLDEN FROG
(PANAMA)

BULLOCK'S
FALSE TOAD
(CHILE)

KIHANSI
SPRAY TOAD
(TANZANIA)

MOUNTAIN
MISTFROG
(AUSTRALIA)

THESE AMPHIBIANS HAVE
LOW POPULATIONS AND COULD
ONE DAY DIE OUT ALTOGETHER.

GLOSSARY

absorb: to take in

ancestor: an animal that lived before others in its family tree

blood vessel: a small tube in an animal's body that carries blood

burrow: a hole made by an animal in which it lives or hides. Also, to make a hole in which to live or hide.

develop: to grow and change

environment: the conditions that surround a living thing and affect the way it lives

evolve: to grow and change over time

extreme: to a very great degree

release: to let something out

research: studying to find something new

shed: to lose fur or skin

tendon: a band of tough tissue that connects muscles and bones

texture: the structure, feel, and appearance of something

FOR MORE INFORMATION

BOOKS

Amstutz, Lisa J. *F Is for Frog: ABCs for Endangered Amphibians.* North Mankato, MN: Capstone Press, 2017.

Ayers, Linda. *Siren Salamander: What Is an Amphibian?* Minneapolis, MN: Cantata Learning, 2016.

WEBSITES

Amphibians
kids.sandiegozoo.org/animals/amphibians
Read more about amphibians here.

Animal Adaptations for Kids
easyscienceforkids.com/animal-adaptations-for-kids-video-for-kids/
Watch a short video about animal adaptations and read more about different kinds of adaptations.

INDEX